CHRISTMAS FAVORITES

Solos and Band Arrangements
Correlated with Essential Elements Band M~~ethod~~

ARRANGED BY
MICHAEL SWEENEY

Welcome to Essential Elements Christmas Favorites! There are two versions of each holiday selection in this versatile book:
1. The SOLO version (with lyrics) appears on the left-hand page.
2. The FULL BAND arrangement appears on the right-hand page.
Use the optional accompaniment tape when playing solos for friends and family. Your director may also use the accompaniment tape in band rehearsals and concerts.

ISBN 978-0-7935-1762-6

HAL•LEONARD® CORPORATION
7777 W. BLUEMOUND RD. P.O. BOX 13819 MILWAUKEE, WI 53213

00862511

JINGLE BELLS

Words and Music by J. PIERPONT
Arranged by MICHAEL SWEENEY

Solo

Introduction

5

Jin - gle Bells,   Jin - gle Bells,   Jin - gle all the way.

Oh what fun it is to ride in a one horse o - pen sleigh!

13

Jin - gle Bells,   Jin - gle Bells,   Jin - gle all the way.

Oh what fun it is to ride in a one horse o - pen sleigh!

21 **Interlude**

Oh what fun it is to ride in a one horse o - pen sleigh!

00862511

JINGLE BELLS

Band Arrangement

Words and Music by J. PIERPONT
Arranged by MICHAEL SWEENEY

00862511

UP ON THE HOUSETOP

Arranged by MICHAEL SWEENEY

Solo

Band Arrangement

Arranged by MICHAEL SWEENEY

Moderately fast

00862511

THE HANUKKAH SONG

Arranged by MICHAEL SWEENEY

Solo

THE HANUKKAH SONG

Band Arrangement

Arranged by MICHAEL SWEENEY

00862511

A HOLLY JOLLY CHRISTMAS

Music and Lyrics by JOHNNY MARKS
Arranged by MICHAEL SWEENEY

Solo

A Holly Jolly Christmas

Music and Lyrics by JOHNNY MARKS
Arranged by MICHAEL SWEENEY

Band Arrangement

WE WISH YOU A MERRY CHRISTMAS

Solo

Arranged by MICHAEL SWEENEY

WE WISH YOU A MERRY CHRISTMAS

Band Arrangement

Arranged by MICHAEL SWEENEY

00862511

FROSTY THE SNOW MAN

Words and Music by STEVE NELSON and JACK ROLLINS
Arranged by MICHAEL SWEENEY

Solo

Introduction

Frost - y, the snow man was a jol - ly hap - py soul, With a

corn cob pipe and a but - ton nose and two eyes made out of coal. Frost - y the

snow man is a fair - y tale they say, He was made of snow but the chil - dren know how he

came to life one day. There must have been some mag - ic in that old silk hat they

found. For when they placed it on his head he be - gan to dance a - round. Oh,

Frost - y the snow man was a - live as he could be And the

chil - dren say he could laugh and play just the same as you and me.

Thump-et - y thump thump, thump-et - y thump thump Look at Frost - y go

Thump - et - y thump thump, thump-et - y thump thump O - ver the hills of snow.

FROSTY THE SNOW MAN

Words and Music by STEVE NELSON and JACK ROLLINS
Arranged by MICHAEL SWEENEY

Band Arrangement

ROCKIN' AROUND
THE CHRISTMAS TREE

Music and Lyrics by JOHNNY MARKS
Arranged by MICHAEL SWEENEY

Solo

ROCKIN' AROUND THE CHRISTMAS TREE

Music and Lyrics by JOHNNY MARKS
Arranged by MICHAEL SWEENEY

Band Arrangement

00862511

JINGLE-BELL ROCK

Words and Music by JOE BEAL and JIM BOOTHE
Arranged by MICHAEL SWEENEY

Solo

Introduction

Jin-gle-bell, Jin-gle-bell, Jin-gle-bell rock Jin-gle-bell swing and Jin-gle-bells ring. Snow-in' and blow-in' up bush-els of fun Now the Jin-gle-hop has be-gun. Jin-gle-bell, Jin-gle-bell, Jin-gle-bell rock Jin-gle-bells chime in Jin-gle-bell time. Danc-in' and pranc-in' in Jin-gle-bell Square In the frost-y air. What a bright time, it's the right time to rock the night a-way. Jin-gle-bell time is a swell time to go glid-in' in a one-horse sleigh. Gid-dy-ap, Jin-gle-horse pick up your feet. Jin-gle a-round the clock. Mix and min-gle in a jin-gl-in' beat. That's the Jin-gle-bell, That's the Jin-gle-bell, That's the Jin-gle-bell rock.

JINGLE-BELL ROCK

**Words and Music by JOE BEAL
and JIM BOOTHE**
Arranged by MICHAEL SWEENEY

Band Arrangement

00862511

RUDOLPH THE RED-NOSED REINDEER

Music and Lyrics by JOHNNY MARKS
Arranged by MICHAEL SWEENEY

Solo

RUDOLPH THE RED-NOSED REINDEER

Music and Lyrics by JOHNNY MARKS
Arranged by MICHAEL SWEENEY

Band Arrangement

LET IT SNOW!
LET IT SNOW! LET IT SNOW!

Words by SAMMY CAHN
Music by JULE STYNE
Arranged by MICHAEL SWEENEY

Solo

LET IT SNOW! LET IT SNOW! LET IT SNOW!

Words by SAMMY CAHN
Music by JULE STYNE
Arranged by MICHAEL SWEENEY

Band Arrangement

00862511

THE CHRISTMAS SONG

Music and Lyric by MEL TORME and ROBERT WELLS

Arranged by MICHAEL SWEENEY

Solo

THE CHRISTMAS SONG

Music and Lyric by MEL TORME and ROBERT WELLS

Band Arrangement

Arranged by MICHAEL SWEENEY